COURAGE

UNDER FIRE

TRUE STORIES OF BRAVERY FROM THE U.S. ARMY, NAVY, AIR FORCE, AND MARINES

BY STEVEN OTFINOSKI, JESSICA GUNDERSON, AND ADAM MILLER

CAPSTONE PRESS
a capstone imprint

Published by Capstone Press,
1710 Roe Crest Drive, North Mankato, Minnesota 56003
www.capstonepub.com

Library of Congress Cataloging-in-Publication Data
Otfinoski, Steven.
  Courage under fire : true stories of bravery from the U.S. Army, Navy, Air
Force, and Marines / by Steven Otfinoski, Jessica Gunderson, and Adam
Miller.
    pages cm
  Includes bibliographical references and index.
  Summary: "Provides gripping accounts of Army, Navy, Air Force, and
Marines servicemen and servicewomen who showed exceptional courage
during combat"—Provided by publisher.
  Audience: Grades 4–6.
  ISBN 978-1-4914-1065-3 (paperback)
1. United States—Armed Forces—Juvenile literature. 2. Soldiers—United
States—Biography—Juvenile literature. 3. Sailors—United States—
Biography—Juvenile literature. 4. Airmen—United States—Biography—
Juvenile literature. 5. Marines—United States—Biography—Juvenile literature.
6. Combat—Juvenile literature. 7. Courage—Juvenile literature. I. Gunderson,
Jessica. II. Miller, Adam, 1970- III. Title. IV. Title: True stories of bravery from
the U.S. Army, Navy, Air Force, and Marines.
  UA23.O84 2015
  355.0092'273—dc23   2014019590

Editorial Credits
Christopher L. Harbo, editor; Veronica Scott, designer; Gene Bentdahl and
Charmaine Whitman, production specialists

Photo Credits
AP Photo: John Moore, 29, 30; Corbis, 42, 45, 61, ACME, 89, 91, Bettmann,
14, 17, 46, 62; Getty Images: AFP/Mehdi Fedouach, 54, Keystone, 88, Mark
Wilson, 48, Museum of Science and Industry, Chicago, 44, Oleg Nikishin, 51,
Pool Photo, 53, Popperfoto, 63, Scott Peterson, 106, Time & Life Pictures/
Dick Swanson, 72, Time & Life Pictures/Frank Scherschel, 66, U.S. Navy, 43;
iStockphotos: lauradyoung, 5 (SS); NARA, 67, 68, U.S. Army Air Forces, 19,
U.S. Army/Lt. Adrian C. Duff, 15, U.S. Marine Corps/SSgt. W. W. Frank, 92,
U.S. Marine Corps, 94, U.S. Navy, 98, U.S. Navy, Office of Public Relations,
40; Newscom: Everett Collection, 9, 22, 60, 86, Fort-Worth Star-Telegram/Paul
Moseley, 55; Shutterstock: Adam Ziaja, cover, 1, Jim Barber, 5 (DSC), Gary
Blakeley, 13, Gavran333, 14, nazlisart, 9, 11, R Carner, 5 (PH, BS), Susan Law
Cain, 12; Smithsonian National Air and Space Museum (WEB10053-2004), 83;
U.S. Air Force photo, 64, 65, 69, 70, 73, 74, 75, 81, 2nd Lt. Keavy Rake, 79, Capt.
Justin T. Watson, 82, Senior Airman Grovert Fuentes-Contreras, 77, Staff Sgt.
Michael B. Keller, 58 (inset), Staff Sgt. Ryan Crane, 3, 58; U.S. Army photo,
25, 28, 52, Private First Class Brandon R. Aird, 6 (inset), Staff Sgt. Adelita
Mead, 6; U.S. Marine Corps photo, 102, 104, Cpl. Andres J. Lugo, 95, Cpl.
Brian J. Slaght, 84 (inset), Cpl. Randall A. Clinton, 100, Cpl. Reece Lodder,
84, Gunnery Sgt. Kevin W. Williams, 109, Lance Cpl. Christofer P. Baines,
97, Sgt. Jeffery Cordero, 96, Staff Sgt. Ryan Smith, 105; U.S. Naval Historical
Center Photograph, 34, 35, 37, 38; U.S. Navy photo, 32, 45, 49 (inset), 56,
MC3 David Smart, 57, MCC Gary A. Prill, 32 (inset); Wikimedia: Claire H.,
11, miscellaneous, 36, NARA/James K. F. Dung, SFC, 24, NARA/U.S. Army
Signal Corps Collection, 18, public domain, 10, U.S. Air Force, 5 (AF DFC) U.S.
Army/Spc. Micah E. Clare, 26, U.S. Army/Spc. Micah E. Clare, 27, U.S. Coast
Guard/CPHOM Robert F. Sargent, 21, U.S. National Guard/Rick Reeves, 8,
U.S. Marine Corps, 101, 108; Wikipedia: DoD, 5, (LOM, MOH, NC, NMCC),
U.S. Air Force, 5 (AFC), U.S. Marine Corps/Sgt. Luis R. Agostini, 107

Design Elements
Shutterstock: Benjamin Haas, Filipchuk Oleg Vasiliovich, locote, Oleg Zabielin,
Petr Vaclavek, rick seeney

Printed in China.
223

STANDING STRONG

The United States Army, Navy, Air Force, and Marines stand together with a common mission. They strive to protect the United States from outside threats. With more than 1.4 million active duty members, the U.S. military takes the fight to our enemies—wherever they may be. From land to sea to air, U.S. servicemen and women protect American freedom.

The U.S. military has roots that run deeper than the country's cornerstones. Since the early days of the Revolutionary War (1775–1783), America's armed forces have marched through history's greatest conflicts. From the first battles with the British to modern warfare in Afghanistan, the U.S. military has always answered the call to action.

In the battlefront stories that follow, the brave actions of dozens of extraordinary heroes come to life. From an Army soldier who fought to the death to protect his fellow soldiers to a Marine who sacrificed himself on a live grenade, you'll witness heroism that goes beyond measure. For when their call to duty came, these soldiers, sailors, and airmen displayed exceptional courage under fire.

MILITARY AWARDS

Medal of Honor:
the highest award for bravery in the U.S. military

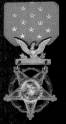

Army

Navy/ Marines

Air Force

Bronze Star:
the fourth-highest award for bravery in the U.S. military

Legion of Merit:
the sixth-highest award for bravery in the U.S. military

Air Force Cross:
the second-highest military award for bravery that is given to members of the Air Force

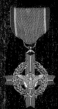

Distinguished Service Cross:
the second-highest military award for bravery that is given to members of the U.S. Army (and Air Force prior to 1960)

Navy Cross:
the second-highest military award for bravery that is given to members of the Navy and Marines

Silver Star:
the third-highest award for bravery in the U.S. military

Purple Heart:
an award given to members of the military wounded by the enemy in combat

Distinguished Flying Cross:
an award given to members of the military who show extraordinary achievement in flight

Navy and Marine Corps Commendation Medal:
an award given to members of the Navy and Marines for sustained acts of heroism and meritorious service

U.S. ARMY TRUE STORIES

THIS WE'LL DEFEND

The Army is the heart and soul of the United States' military. As the largest branch of the military, it has more than 500,000 soldiers ready for action. Army soldiers take the fight to enemies on the ground. They also guard and protect U.S. bases and installations around the world.

The Army also is the oldest branch of the U.S. military. It was founded on June 14, 1775, by the Second Continental Congress. The branch's name at that time was the Continental Army. Led by George Washington, the Army won America's independence from Great Britain during the Revolutionary War. Since then the Army has fought in every war the United States has entered.

While the Army's weapons and technology have changed over time, the courage of its soldiers has stayed the same. The Army's motto is "This We'll Defend." Army soldiers have bravely defended the United States for more than 200 years.

THE CIVIL WAR

DATES: 1861–1865

THE COMBATANTS: UNION (NORTHERN STATES) VS. CONFEDERATE STATES OF AMERICA (SOUTHERN STATES)

THE VICTOR: UNION

CASUALTIES: UNION–364,511 DEAD; CONFEDERATE–164,821 DEAD

Sergeant William Carney holds the flag high as the 54th Massachusetts Colored Infantry attacks Fort Wagner.

SERGEANT WILLIAM CARNEY

During the Civil War, Sergeant William Carney served in the Union's 54th Massachusetts Colored Infantry. The 54th was the first African-American regiment sent into battle. The regiment's very first taste of action came at James Island, South Carolina, on July 16, 1863. Two days later the regiment's soldiers arrived on Morris Island in Charleston Harbor. The 54th volunteered to lead the charge on the Confederate's heavily defended Fort Wagner.

During the attack Carney and his fellow soldiers rushed uphill to the fort. John Wall, the color sergeant, ran beside him carrying the Union flag. When Wall got hit by a bullet, Carney immediately dropped his gun. He grabbed the flag from the dying soldier and dashed toward the fort.

Bullets whizzed by him. Two bullets struck his leg and one hit his right arm. Badly wounded, he finally reached the fort's wall and planted the flag in the sand.

Unable to take the fort, Union forces retreated. But Carney refused to leave the flag behind. Other soldiers tried to take the flag from him as they helped him to safety, but he wouldn't let it go. Stumbling and crawling,

Carney with the flag he saved

he finally made it back to the Union ranks. When he arrived he told his regiment, "The old Flag never touched the ground."

Nearly half of the 54th's 600 soldiers died in the attack on Fort Wagner. Many years after the war, Carney was honored for his bravery. He earned the Medal of Honor. He was the first African-American to receive the honor.

SERGEANT RICHARD KIRKLAND

The Angel of Mayre's Heights statue

On December 13, 1862, the Civil War's Battle of Fredericksburg entered its third day. Union forces charged across a field at Mayre's Heights in Virginia. Meanwhile, Confederate troops awaited them behind a long stone wall. The Confederates mowed down wave after wave of Union soldiers. By dawn on December 14, hundreds of wounded Union soldiers cried out for help. Confederate sergeant Richard Kirkland asked Brigadier General Joseph Kershaw if he could take them water. Kershaw refused, but Kirkland kept asking.

The general finally let him go. Kirkland filled every canteen he could find with water. Then he crawled over the wall and crept toward the wounded soldiers. Union sharpshooters thought Kirkland was stealing from dead soldiers. They fired on him. But they stopped when they realized he had come to help. General Kershaw later wrote: "For an hour and a half did this ministering angel pursue his labor of mercy ... until he had relieved all of the wounded on that part of the field." Today a statue of "The Angel of Mayre's Heights" stands near the wall Kirkland bravely crossed.

WORLD WAR I

DATES: 1914–1918

THE COMBATANTS: ALLIES (MAIN COUNTRIES: GREAT BRITAIN, FRANCE, ITALY, RUSSIA, UNITED STATES) VS. CENTRAL POWERS (MAIN COUNTRIES: GERMANY, AUSTRIA-HUNGARY, BULGARIA, OTTOMAN EMPIRE)

THE VICTOR: ALLIES

CASUALTIES: ALLIES—5,142,631 DEAD; CENTRAL POWERS—3,386,200 DEAD

American soldiers in the trenches of France during World War I

SERGEANT ALVIN YORK

    Sergeant Alvin York was born on a farm in the mountains of Tennessee. When the United States entered World War I in 1917, York refused to join the Army. His religion was against war. But the U.S. government did not recognize his church. York was drafted and reluctantly went off to fight in France.

    On October 8, 1918, York and a group of 16 American soldiers set out to capture a railroad in France's Argonne Forest. German machine gun teams spotted the Americans as they were coming around a hill and opened fire. Nine soldiers on the right flank were killed or wounded. York was hidden from view on the left flank. He started firing back. He later described what happened next. "I was right out in the open and the machine guns were spitting fire and cutting up all around me something awful. But they didn't seem to be able to hit me." York's rifle grew hot in his hands. His ammunition was almost gone, but he kept firing. By the time the smoke cleared, nine German machine gunners lay dead. York's courage inspired his remaining comrades. They took out 25 more Germans.

The German commander thought he was up against a large American force and surrendered. York and the remaining American soldiers captured 132 German soldiers. He and his men marched their prisoners 10 miles (16 kilometers) to the American headquarters in Varennes. York returned home a hero and received the Medal of Honor for his actions.

Sergeant Alvin York

CORPORAL DONALD CALL

Donald Call was a stage actor before World War I. However, no role he played was more dramatic than the one he filled on the battlefield near Varennes, France.

On September 26, 1918, Call and an officer were using their tank to fight German machine gun nests. Suddenly an artillery shell blew half the tank's turret off. Gas filled the tank, making it difficult to breathe. Call scrambled out of the tank and ran for safety.

But when Call turned around, the officer wasn't behind him. Without a second thought, Call dashed back to the tank. Dodging enemy gunfire and falling shells, he climbed back into the tank. He found the officer alive but unable to move. He pulled him from the tank. Then he carried him 1 mile (1.6 km) through the battlefield while snipers fired at them. After the war Call received the Medal of Honor for his courage.

American tank in World War I

PRIVATE HENRY JOHNSON

Private Henry Johnson served in France during World War I. One night while he was on guard duty, the Germans attacked. Sniper bullets whizzed by Johnson and Private Needham Roberts. Suddenly the "snip-snip" sound of someone cutting through the protective fence floated out of the darkness. Johnson realized the Germans were closing in. He sent Roberts back to warn their camp. But a German grenade wounded Roberts' hip and arm. Roberts crawled back to Johnson for safety.

Johnson told Roberts to stay down and hand him grenades. He hurled every grenade they had, but the Germans kept coming. Johnson was shot in the head and lip, but he fired his rifle until it jammed. More bullets pierced his body. Johnson swung his rifle like a club at the advancing Germans. When they knocked him down, he jumped up with his knife in hand. He stabbed at Germans trying to take Roberts prisoner. Finally, French and American soldiers arrived and forced the Germans to retreat. Johnson passed out and was taken to a field hospital. Doctors discovered 21 wounds on his body. The next day, soldiers learned Johnson had taken out four Germans and wounded 10 others.

Private Henry Johnson's hand-to-hand combat with the Germans earned him the nickname "Black Death" during World War I.

Both Johnson and Roberts survived the attack. For their courage, they became the first American privates to be awarded the Croix du Guerre. It is France's highest military honor. For his fighting skills, Henry Johnson earned the nickname "Black Death."

WORLD WAR II

DATES: 1939–1945

THE COMBATANTS: ALLIES (MAIN COUNTRIES: GREAT BRITAIN, FRANCE, RUSSIA, UNITED STATES) VS. AXIS POWERS (MAIN COUNTRIES: GERMANY, ITALY, JAPAN)

THE VICTOR: ALLIES

CASUALTIES: ALLIES—14,141,544 DEAD; AXIS—5,634,232 DEAD

American troops approach Omaha Beach on a landing craft during the D-Day invasion on June 6, 1944.

CAPTAIN JOSEPH DAWSON

June 6, 1944, was the turning point of World War II. Thousands of American soldiers landed on the beaches along France's Normandy coast during the D-Day invasion. Their goal was to take the country back from the Germans. Many heroes stormed the beaches that day. One of them was Captain Joseph Dawson.

When Dawson and his 1st Infantry Division landed on Omaha Beach, German gunners awaited them. The Germans rained down firepower. Bullets cut the air around Dawson and his men. But he charged ahead, scrambling up the beach with his men in tow. Along the way, Dawson was shot in the knee and right leg. Still, he pressed forward. As they approached the crest of a hill, Dawson heard German voices. "I could now hear the Germans talking in the machine gun nest immediately above me," he later explained. Despite his wounds, Dawson tossed two grenades into the nest. The blasts silenced the machine gun fire.

By the end of the day, Dawson and his men had gone farther inland than any other American soldiers. For his bravery and leadership that day, Dawson received the Distinguished Service Cross.

But Dawson's bravery during the war didn't end on Omaha Beach. As the Americans pushed through France toward Paris, Dawson continued to fight. He rescued an American platoon ambushed by enemies.

Later in 1944 Dawson's company seized a ridge overlooking the German city of Aachen. Wave after wave of German soldiers attacked the ridge. But Dawson and his men refused to give up. They defended the ridge for 39 days. Their courage allowed other American troops to take Aachen. It was the first German city to fall to the Allies in the war. The ridge was later named "Dawson's Ridge" in his honor.

The U.S. Army's 1st Division slogs through the water before storming Omaha Beach.

THE KOREAN WAR

DATES: 1950–1953

THE COMBATANTS: UNITED STATES, SOUTH KOREA, AND UNITED NATIONS (UN) vs. NORTH KOREA AND CHINA

THE VICTOR: NO VICTOR; THE UN AND NORTH KOREA SIGNED A TRUCE, BUT NO PERMANENT PEACE TREATY WAS EVER SIGNED BY NORTH KOREA AND SOUTH KOREA

CASUALTIES: UNITED STATES, UN, AND SOUTH KOREA—256,631 DEAD; CHINA AND NORTH KOREA—ESTIMATED 1,006,000 DEAD

American soldiers hunker down in trenches during the Korean War.

PRIVATE HERBERT PILILAAU

Herbert Pililaau was a gentle soul from Hawaii. He was also a fine singer who played the ukulele. But while serving his country in the Korean War, he fought fiercely to protect his fellow soldiers.

Private Pililaau served in a platoon stationed on "Heartbreak Ridge" near Pia-ri, Korea. On September 17, 1951, a huge wave of North Korean soldiers tried to take the ridge from the Americans. Pililaau and his platoon fought off the enemy until they were almost out of ammunition. Officers ordered the men to move to a safer location. Pililaau volunteered to stay behind to provide cover fire for the retreating soldiers. When his gun ran out of bullets, Pililaau began lobbing grenades at the enemy. When the grenades ran out, he pulled out his knife. He fought the attackers in hand-to-hand combat. He finally swung at them with his fists until they overwhelmed him.

Later Pililaau's platoon members retook the area and recovered his body. The bodies of more than 40 enemy soldiers surrounded him. Pililaau is believed to have killed most—if not all—of them himself.

Pililaau received the Medal of Honor posthumously. It was given for "conspicuous [outstanding] gallantry [bravery] ... at the risk of his life above and beyond the call of duty."

THE VIETNAM WAR

DATES: 1959–1975

THE COMBATANTS: United States, South Vietnam, and their allies vs. North Vietnam and its allies

THE VICTOR: North Vietnam

CASUALTIES: United States—58,220 dead; South Vietnam—estimated 200,000 to 250,000 dead; North Vietnam—estimated 1.1 million dead

U.S. Army helicopters pick up soldiers after a mission in South Vietnam.

SERGEANT BILLY WALKABOUT

Helping wounded soldiers while being seriously injured is the mark of a true hero. On November 20, 1968, Sergeant Billy Walkabout, who was a Cherokee Indian, and 12 other soldiers came under heavy fire behind enemy lines. One man was seriously wounded. Walkabout gave the man first aid and radioed for a helicopter.

While loading the injured soldier onto the chopper, a land mine blew up. The blast killed three men. The rest, including Walkabout, were wounded. But Walkabout still rushed from man to man, treating their wounds.

As more helicopters landed, Walkabout helped load the wounded into them. He refused to be taken to safety until all of his fellow soldiers were safely aboard the choppers.

Walkabout's heroism earned him a Distinguished Service Cross. In addition he earned a Purple Heart, five Silver Stars, and five Bronze Stars during his 23 months in Vietnam. He was one of the most decorated soldiers to serve in the war.

OPERATION ENDURING FREEDOM

DATES: 2001–PRESENT

THE COMBATANTS: AFGHANISTAN GOVERNMENT, THE UNITED STATES AND ITS COALITION FORCES VS. AL-QAIDA TERRORIST ORGANIZATION AND THE TALIBAN, AN ISLAMIC GROUP THAT SUPPORTS AL-QAIDA

THE VICTOR: CONFLICT ONGOING

CASUALTIES: AMERICAN AND COALITION FORCES (THROUGH DECEMBER 6, 2012)–3,215 DEAD; AFGHAN CIVILIANS (REPORTED FROM JANUARY 2007 TO JUNE 2012)–13,009 DEAD; TALIBAN AND AL-QAIDA–NUMBER UNKNOWN

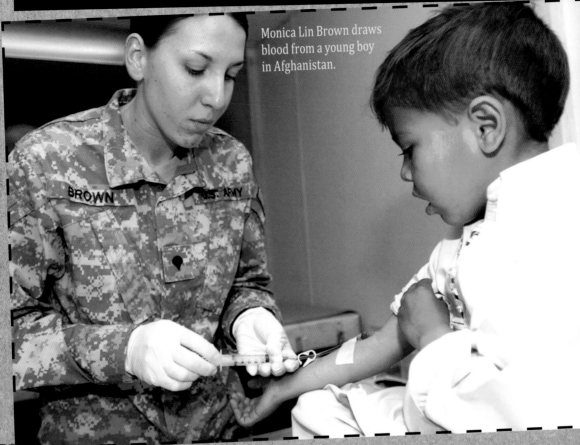

Monica Lin Brown draws blood from a young boy in Afghanistan.

ARMY SPECIALIST MONICA LIN BROWN

On April 25, 2007, Army medic Monica Lin Brown was on a security patrol in Afghanistan's Paktika province. Without warning, the enemy attacked her convoy. An explosive hit the Humvee behind hers. Brown and Staff Sergeant Jose Santos rushed from their vehicle to the burning Humvee. Five soldiers poured out of the vehicle. Two were seriously injured. While the enemy fired on them, Brown and Santos helped the group to another vehicle. "Somewhere in the mix, we started taking mortar rounds," recalled Brown. "It became a huge commotion, but all I could let myself think about were my patients."

Bullets flew everywhere as Brown prepared the men for helicopter rescue. At last the enemy retreated. Brown helped the wounded men to the arriving helicopter. Without her aid they may not have survived.

For her bravery Brown received a Silver Star. She was only the second woman since World War II to receive this honor.

STAFF SERGEANT CLINTON ROMESHA

Staff Sergeant Clinton Romesha was stationed at a remote valley outpost in Afghanistan's Nuristan province. On October 3, 2009, 300 Taliban fighters attacked the outpost with machine guns and rocket grenades.

Romesha returned fire. He shot one machine gun team with a sniper's rifle. Then a rocket grenade struck the electric generator he was hiding behind. Shrapnel wounded his neck, shoulder, and arms, but he kept fighting. He gathered a team of five men, and they counterattacked. Romesha radioed the location of the enemy to the operations center. They sent in aircraft that took out another 30 Taliban fighters.

Eight Americans were killed and 22 wounded in the fierce fighting. But thanks to Romesha, the outpost was not taken. On February 11, 2013, he was awarded the Medal of Honor.

OPERATION IRAQI FREEDOM

DATES: 2003–2011

THE COMBATANTS: THE UNITED STATES AND COALITION FORCES VS. IRAQ, FIRST THE GOVERNMENT OF SADDAM HUSSEIN AND THEN INSURGENTS

THE VICTOR: THE UNITED STATES DEFEATED SADDAM HUSSEIN IN 2003 BUT THEN FACED STIFF FIGHTING FROM INSURGENTS UNTIL ITS WITHDRAWAL IN 2011

CASUALTIES: AMERICAN AND COALITION FORCES—4,804 DEAD; IRAQI SOLDIERS AND INSURGENTS—ESTIMATED MORE THAN 30,000 DEAD

Smoke billows from a burning car on a bridge controlled by Army forces in Al Hindiyah, Iraq.

CAPTAIN CHRIS CARTER

On March 31, 2003, the main U.S. forces invading Iraq prepared to enter the Karbala Gap. This 1-mile- (1.6-km-) wide passage would bring troops closer to the capital city of Baghdad. But the military wanted to fool the Iraqis into thinking they were moving elsewhere. Captain Chris Carter and his company had orders to enter the city of Al Hindiyah to take control of a bridge. Carter's company carried out the diversion with tanks and other armed vehicles. Iraqi troops fired machine guns and hurled grenades as the troops passed.

Captain Chris Carter calls for an armored ambulance to come to the aid of an injured Iraqi woman on March 31, 2003.

Carter held his position in front of the bridge for several hours. Then a soldier spotted an elderly Iraqi woman lying in the middle of the bridge. She had gotten caught up in the battle, and she was waving for help. Carter leaped into action. He ordered an armored vehicle to move toward the bridge while he and two other soldiers followed on foot.

When they reached the woman, Carter threw a smoke grenade so the enemy couldn't see them clearly. The captain knelt by the woman and gave her water. He discovered she was bleeding and radioed for an armored ambulance. When it arrived, the two soldiers carried the woman to safety. Carter provided cover by firing at the enemy.

Later Carter was asked why he saved the woman in the middle of fierce fighting. He said he came to Iraq to fight "... for the people. To leave her out on that bridge would have gone against the grain of why we are here."

U.S. NAVY TRUE STORIES

NOT SELF BUT COUNTRY

Throughout history a country's might has often been measured by its navy's strength. Serving at sea, in the air, and on land, the U.S. Navy is the most powerful naval force in the world. Its mission is to be a "global force for good." The Navy's goal is to prevent conflicts, win wars, and maintain freedom of the seas.

The Navy's history stretches all the way back to the Revolutionary War. At that time the Continental Congress voted to send two armed ships to sea to stop the British Navy. Called the Continental Navy, the growing fleet helped win American independence. Since that time the Navy has fought in every U.S. war. During World War II, the Navy helped defeat the Japanese in the Pacific. In the Vietnam War, the Navy formed special operations teams called SEALs. These teams carried out dangerous, secret missions, and still do today.

The Navy doesn't have an official motto. But its sailors uphold the idea of "not self but country." They answer any call for combat support, rescue help, and disaster relief. Their bravery, selflessness, and honor is at the heart of the U.S. Navy.

THE CIVIL WAR

Dates: 1861–1865

The Combatants: Union (Northern states) vs. Confederate States of America (Southern states)

The Victor: Union

Casualties: Union–364,511 dead; Confederate–164,821 dead

The USS *Monitor* (front) and the CSS *Virginia* fire on each other during the Battle of Hampton Roads in 1862.

LIEUTENANT JOHN WORDEN

In March 1862 Union Lieutenant John Lorimer Worden sailed the ironclad USS *Monitor* to Hampton Roads, Virginia. He arrived to find the Confederate ironclad *Virginia* attacking the Union warship *Minnesota*.

Worden moved the *Monitor* between the two ships. The two ironclads pounded each other with shells. As Worden raced between the deck and the pilothouse, he ordered his crew to keep firing.

During the battle Worden peered between the pilothouse bars when a shell exploded. Metal fragments spun through the air. Worden toppled backward, screaming, "My eyes! I am blind!" Despite his pain, he ordered his helmsman to steer away from the *Virginia*.

The crew helped Worden to his cabin. As a doctor plucked iron shards from his eyes, Worden placed Lieutenant Samuel Greene in charge of the *Monitor*. He told Greene, "I cannot see, but don't mind me. Save the *Minnesota* if you can."

The *Monitor* protected the *Minnesota* from further damage, and the *Virginia* left the battle. Worden recovered his eyesight and received the rank of commander. Since then the Navy has named several ships after him.

LIEUTENANT ROBERT MINOR

During the Battle of Hampton Roads, the Union warship *Congress* surrendered to the Confederates. But the Union ship still sat in the water. Onboard the Confederate ship *Virginia*, Lieutenant Robert Dabney Minor heard his captain say the *Congress* must be burned. He didn't want the Northerners to retake the damaged ship.

Minor immediately offered to lead a small group to burn the ship. He and several other sailors set off for the *Congress* in a small gunboat. As they neared the ship, a hail of gunfire broke out from shore. "The way the balls danced around my little boat and crew was lively beyond measure," Minor recalled. Through the shower of bullets, Minor urged his men on. Suddenly, pain ripped through him. A bullet had pierced his chest and he dropped to the bottom of the boat.

With their leader down, Minor's crew panicked. Despite his bleeding chest, Minor pulled himself to his feet. He calmed the men until a Confederate ship came to their aid.

The USS *Congress* (right) sails near Naples, Italy, prior to its involvement in the U.S. Civil War.

Meanwhile the *Virginia* drew close to the *Congress* and set it on fire. Minor recovered and later served as flag lieutenant of the James River Squadron. This squadron was one of the Confederacy's eight major naval forces.

WORLD WAR I

Dates: 1914–1918

The Combatants: Allies (main countries: Great Britain, France, Italy, Russia, United States) vs. Central Powers (main countries: Germany, Austria-Hungary, Bulgaria, Ottoman Empire)

The Victor: Allies

Casualties: Allies–5,142,631 dead; Central Powers–3,386,200 dead

Lieutenant Joel T. Boone (second from right) stands with fellow servicemen during World War I.

LIEUTENANT JOEL BOONE

The Navy Medical Corps often serves with Army and Marine units. Although not in direct combat, Medical Corps members often risk their lives to tend the wounded. During World War I, Corps member Lieutenant Joel Thompson Boone did just that.

In July 1918, near Vierzy, France, American and French forces clashed with the German army. As a Navy surgeon, Boone was attached to the 6th Marine Regiment. While his group moved into an open field, heavy artillery and gunfire bombarded it. Marines fell by the dozen. Through the gunfire, Boone dashed onto the battlefield, medical supplies in tow. Despite explosions and whizzing bullets, he worked furiously to save wounded soldiers.

When Boone's medical supplies ran low, he ran across the battlefield for more. Shells filled with poisonous gas exploded nearby, but Boone kept going. After gathering more supplies, he returned to the battlefield. When his supplies ran low again, he repeated the dangerous trip. American casualties were heavy, but Boone saved many lives.

For his heroism Boone received the Medal of Honor. He went on to serve in World War II and the Korean War. He became the nation's most decorated medical officer. He earned the Army's Distinguished Service Cross, a Silver Star, and many other honors.

WORLD WAR II

DATES: 1939–1945

THE COMBATANTS: ALLIES (MAIN COUNTRIES: GREAT BRITAIN, FRANCE, RUSSIA, UNITED STATES) VS. AXIS POWERS (MAIN COUNTRIES: GERMANY, ITALY, JAPAN)

THE VICTOR: ALLIES

CASUALTIES: ALLIES—14,141,544 DEAD; AXIS—5,634,232 DEAD

Billowing plumes of smoke rise from the USS *West Virginia* during the attack on Pearl Harbor on December 7, 1941.

MESS ATTENDANT SECOND CLASS DORIS MILLER

In 1939 Doris "Dorie" Miller joined the U.S. Navy as a mess attendant. This position was one of only a few open to African-Americans at that time. By 1941 he was assigned to the USS *West Virginia*, stationed in Pearl Harbor, Hawaii.

On the morning of December 7, 1941, Miller was collecting laundry when the ship's alarm blared. He raced to the upper deck. Overhead nearly 200 Japanese fighter planes circled the sky. They rained bombs down on the *West Virginia* and the other U.S. battleships. Pearl Harbor was under attack.

Miller rushed through the smoke. Because of his large size and strength, he was ordered to help move the wounded away from the burning upper deck. Suddenly, a lieutenant called him to help the ship's injured captain. With two others, Miller carried the captain away from the smoke and deck fires.

The lieutenant then ordered Miller to man an antiaircraft machine gun. Without any training on the weapon, Miller began firing at the planes. "It wasn't hard," he recalled. "I just pulled the trigger and she worked fine. I had watched the others with these guns."

Doris "Dorie" Miller

The Japanese planes zoomed close, and Miller continued to fire. For fifteen minutes he pounded ammunition into the sky. Bombs soared above him, oily fires sprang up on the deck, and thick smoke swirled about the ship. Water whooshed across the deck as sailors rushed to put out the fires. Despite the chaos, Miller kept to his post until he ran out of ammunition. Soon he heard the call to abandon the sinking *West Virginia*.

Of the 1,541 sailors onboard the *West Virginia*, 130 were killed and 52 were wounded. For his brave actions, Miller became the first African-American to receive the Navy Cross. He also received the Purple Heart. He died in 1943 while onboard the aircraft carrier *Liscome Bay* that was under attack from a Japanese submarine. In June 1973 the USS *Miller* was named in his honor.

USS *West Virginia*

LIEUTENANT ALBERT DAVID

During World War II, the Atlantic Ocean swarmed with German U-boat submarines. On June 4, 1944, a group of U.S. warships located Germany's *U-505*. By pounding the water with depth charges, they forced the sub to the surface. As Germans leaped from the U-boat, Lieutenant Albert Leroy David sprung into action. He and a team of sailors from the USS *Pillsbury* scrambled onto a small motorboat. They sped toward the sub and jumped to its slippery deck. David knew Germans could be hiding below or the sub could explode or sink at any moment. But despite the risks, he plunged down the submarine's hatch.

The sub was empty but sinking fast. Swells of water broke across the deck and whooshed down the hatch. David called to the men on deck to close the hatch. Then he raced toward the radio room to retrieve the enemy's secret codes and charts.

As David and his men prowled the belly of the sub, another group arrived to help keep it afloat. *U-505* was the Navy's first captured enemy vessel at sea since 1815. For his brave actions, David was awarded the Medal of Honor.

The USS *Pillsbury* sits alongside the German submarine *U-505* on June 4, 1944.

U.S. sailors stand on the deck of *U-505* shortly after capturing it.

THE VIETNAM WAR

Dates: 1959–1975

The Combatants: United States, South Vietnam, and their allies vs. North Vietnam and its allies

The Victor: North Vietnam

Casualties: United States—58,220 dead; South Vietnam—estimated 200,000 to 250,000 dead; North Vietnam—estimated 1.1 million dead

Navy SEALs watch an explosion destroy an enemy bunker during the Vietnam War.

PETTY OFFICER MICHAEL THORNTON

In October 1972 Petty Officer Michael E. Thornton was part of a Navy SEAL team on a secret mission behind enemy lines. Its goal was to cut off the North Vietnamese Army's (NVA) supply route.

As the team moved inland from the seashore, the enemy peppered them with gunfire. Then a grenade landed near Thornton. He tossed it between himself and the enemy several times before it exploded nearby. Shrapnel raked his back, but he was able to regroup with his team behind a sand dune. When Thornton got there, he was told team member Thomas Norris had been shot dead.

Thornton didn't hesitate. He raced to Norris' body, lifted it over his shoulders, and ran. The NVA chased at full speed, shooting wildly. An explosion knocked Thornton to the ground, and he lost his grip on Norris' body. As Thornton crawled toward him, he heard a voice say his name. To his surprise, Norris was still alive!

Thornton grabbed Norris again and rushed into the water. He put his life jacket on Norris, strapped him to his back, and swam with all his might. After hours of swimming, a U.S. boat finally rescued them. Thomas Norris survived his wounds. Michael Thornton received the Medal of Honor for risking his life to save his teammate.

OPERATION ENDURING FREEDOM

DATES: 2001–PRESENT

THE COMBATANTS: AFGHANISTAN GOVERNMENT, THE UNITED STATES AND ITS COALITION FORCES VS. AL-QAIDA TERRORIST ORGANIZATION AND THE TALIBAN, AN ISLAMIC GROUP THAT SUPPORTS AL-QAIDA

THE VICTOR: CONFLICT ONGOING

CASUALTIES: AMERICAN AND COALITION FORCES (THROUGH DECEMBER 6, 2012)–3,215 DEAD; AFGHAN CIVILIANS (REPORTED FROM JANUARY 2007 TO JUNE 2012)–13,009 DEAD; TALIBAN AND AL-QAIDA–NUMBER UNKNOWN

Lieutenant Michael Murphy

Maureen Murphy holds the Medal of Honor awarded to her husband, Michael, after his death in Afghanistan.

LIEUTENANT MICHAEL MURPHY

On June 27, 2005, a helicopter dropped Lieutenant Michael Murphy, and three other Navy SEALs, into a mountainous region in Afghanistan. Their mission was to find the hideout of Mullah Ahmad Shah. He led a terrorist group called the Mountain Tigers.

As Murphy scanned the mountainside with binoculars, he saw 30 to 40 armed Taliban fighters pointing rifles in their direction. The SEALs were trapped. Gunfire rang out as the enemy closed in. The SEALs bounded down the mountain, shooting back at the Taliban fighters. A bullet smashed into Murphy's stomach, but he continued to fight. He called to his team to keep moving.

After an hour of fighting, one SEAL was dead and the rest severely injured. Murphy tried to radio for help but he couldn't get through. He knew he needed to find a signal to save his men. He ran out into open ground, in plain sight of the enemy. Pelted with bullets, he managed to contact headquarters before a shot pierced his back, killing him.

Murphy's brave actions led to the rescue of his last surviving teammate, Marcus Luttrell. Murphy posthumously received the Medal of Honor for his actions. He was also awarded the Silver Star and the Purple Heart.

CHIEF PETTY OFFICER STEPHEN BASS

In November 2001 Taliban prisoners overtook a fortress near Mazar-e-Sharif, Afghanistan. Chief Petty Officer Stephen Bass, a Navy SEAL, joined an American and British rescue team to recover two Americans trapped inside. One was believed to be injured and possibly even dead.

Under a rain of bullets and the thunder of grenades, Bass quickly made his way into the fortress. He reached an active minefield and, despite the danger, crossed it to reach the heart of the fortress. When he saw that one American was alive, Bass dropped down and crawled toward him. But the enemy fire was too dangerous. It forced Bass to turn back.

Bass reported the location of the uninjured American. The team made a plan to rescue him. But they made no plans to recover the other American, believing him dead. Bass couldn't leave without knowing for sure if the man was dead. As night fell he went back inside alone. Enemy gunfire greeted him, but he continued forward, firing back.

When he ran out of ammunition, he grabbed weapons from the bodies of Taliban fighters and used them to fight back. At last he reached the second American. Only when he knew for sure that the American was dead did he retreat from the fortress. For his courageous attempts to rescue the trapped Americans, Bass received a Navy Cross.

U.S. soldiers take cover during an explosion prior to battling Taliban forces in a fortress near Mazar-e-Sharif, Afghanistan, in November 2001.

SENIOR CHIEF PETTY OFFICER BRITT SLABINSKI

In March 2002 Senior Chief Petty Officer Britt Slabinski led a team of SEALs to rescue a teammate from enemy territory in the Afghan mountains. When the SEALs jumped from the helicopter, blasts of gunfire surrounded them. The snow-covered Takur Ghar mountaintop crawled with enemy forces. Slabinski and the SEALs fired back, killing several enemy fighters. During the fighting Slabinski alerted air support to the enemy's position on the mountaintop.

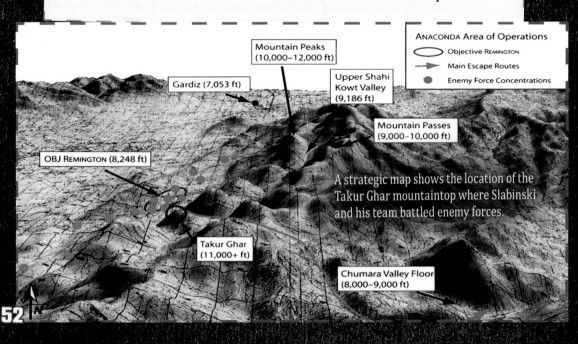

Mountain Peaks
(10,000–12,000 ft)

ANACONDA Area of Operations

⬭ Objective REMINGTON

→ Main Escape Routes

● Enemy Force Concentrations

Gardiz (7,053 ft)

Upper Shahi Kowt Valley (9,186 ft)

Mountain Passes (9,000–10,000 ft)

OBJ REMINGTON (8,248 ft)

A strategic map shows the location of the Takur Ghar mountaintop where Slabinski and his team battled enemy forces.

Takur Ghar (11,000+ ft)

Chumara Valley Floor (8,000–9,000 ft)

A CH-47 Chinook helicopter lands in the Afghan mountains in March 2002.

In the gunfight two SEALs were wounded, and Slabinski knew they could not continue the rescue mission. He hoisted one wounded man into his arms and trekked down the mountain, dodging enemy bullets. Through waist-high snow and bitter cold, he and his team carried the wounded SEALs until a rescue helicopter came to their aid.

Both injured SEALs survived. Slabinski received a Navy Cross for alerting forces to the enemy's position and saving his wounded men.

OPERATION IRAQI FREEDOM

DATES: 2003–2011

THE COMBATANTS: THE UNITED STATES AND COALITION FORCES VS. IRAQ, FIRST THE GOVERNMENT OF SADDAM HUSSEIN AND THEN INSURGENTS

THE VICTOR: THE UNITED STATES DEFEATED SADDAM HUSSEIN IN 2003 BUT THEN FACED STIFF FIGHTING FROM INSURGENTS UNTIL ITS WITHDRAWAL IN 2011

CASUALTIES: AMERICAN AND COALITION FORCES—4,804 DEAD; IRAQI SOLDIERS AND INSURGENTS—ESTIMATED MORE THAN 30,000 DEAD

U.S. Marines patrol a street in Fallujah, Iraq, in 2004.

SEAL TEAM 3 CHIEF CHRIS KYLE

During Operation Iraqi Freedom, Navy SEAL Chris Kyle became the deadliest sniper in U.S. history. His courage matched his sniper skills in Fallujah, Iraq, in 2004. One day while perched on a rooftop, he eyed the streets for enemy activity. As he peered through his gun's scope, the sound of gunfire filled the air.

Kyle left his position and sprinted down the street. He found a group of Marines who told him the insurgents had trapped some of their men. Kyle raced in their direction. Insurgents fired at him, and he fired back. When he rounded a corner, he spotted four soldiers huddled near a wall. He told them to run while he covered them. As the men fled, Kyle noticed a Marine sprawled on the ground. The soldier had been shot in both legs. Kyle grabbed him by his body armor and dragged him as he dashed for safety.

As he fled, a grenade explosion knocked pieces of wall onto Kyle and injured his leg. But he kept running until he and the injured Marine reached shelter. Kyle was awarded a Bronze Star for his bravery in combat. He went on to receive several more Bronze and Silver Stars for his courageous service.

COMMANDER LENORA LANGLAIS

In 2006 Commander Lenora Langlais arrived in Iraq as part of the Navy Medical Corps. On April 7 she was walking at the airbase when enemy bombs dropped from the sky. Sand swirled into the air from the explosions. As Langlais ran for cover, a bomb burst directly above her. Chunks of shrapnel slammed into her neck and face. She dropped to the ground, blood streaming from her neck. A medical team rushed her to the trauma center and quickly operated.

After the operation Langlais refused to go to another hospital for better care. As the most experienced nurse on the airbase, she knew her help was needed. Despite her injuries she helped a patient who was having an allergic reaction to medication. Langlais received a Purple Heart for her service.

Langlais speaks with high school students at a Navy training program in 2009.

U.S. AIR FORCE TRUE STORIES

DAWN OF THE AIR FORCE

The Air Force is the U.S. military's youngest branch. It started in 1907 as the Aeronautical Division of the Army Signal Corps. This division took charge of military balloons and other air machines. Within one year the division tested its first airplane.

Although the Aeronautical Division started small, wars soon brought rapid growth. Just before World War I, the division became the Aviation Section. Then in 1918 America's air forces were renamed the Air Service of the U.S. Army. During nine months of World War I, Air Service pilots shot down 756 enemy aircraft.

By World War II, the Air Service became the Air Corps. It included about 26,500 men and 2,200 aircraft. Then in 1942 the War Department changed the Air Corps into the Army Air Forces. By the end of World War II, more than 2 million men and women and 63,700 aircraft served this huge organization.

On September 18, 1947, the Army Air Forces changed names one last time. The U.S. Air Force finally became its own military branch. But through its long history, one thing has not changed. Its members have served bravely and have taken part in every U.S. war.

WORLD WAR I

Dates: 1914–1918

The Combatants: Allies (main countries: Great Britain, France, Italy, Russia, United States) vs. Central Powers (main countries: Germany, Austria-Hungary, Bulgaria, Ottoman Empire)

The Victor: Allies

Casualties: Allies—5,142,631 dead; Central Powers—3,386,200 dead

Lieutenant Frank Luke Jr. stands beside one of the German observation balloons he shot down on September 18, 1918.

SECOND LIEUTENANT FRANK LUKE JR.

The United States entered World War I in April 1917. Shortly after, Frank Luke Jr. joined the U.S. Army Signal Corps' Aviation Section. In July 1918 he went to France to fly in the 27th Aero Squadron.

Luke's squadron had orders to destroy German observation balloons. These balloons helped the Germans see the battlefields below and plan their ground attacks. Luke and his friend Lieutenant Joseph Frank Wehner worked together on these daredevil missions. Luke attacked the balloons while Wehner defended him from enemy planes. The two ducked and dodged their way around German fighter planes. During seven days in September, Luke shot down 13 enemy aircraft. Then on September 18, Wehner and Luke got caught in a dogfight. Wehner attacked the German fighter, allowing Luke to take out his target. But the fighter shot down Wehner, killing him.

Losing his partner made Luke more determined on his missions than ever. Eleven days later he hunted down three more German balloons. He quickly shot down the first two. After taking out the last balloon, a German soldier fired from a distant hill. The bullet gravely wounded Luke, forcing him to land behind enemy lines. Drawing his gun, Luke took out several German soldiers before dying. For his courage Luke was posthumously awarded the Medal of Honor. The Luke Air Force Base in Arizona was also named after him.

Frank Luke Jr. with his

WORLD WAR II

DATES: 1939–1945

THE COMBATANTS: ALLIES (MAIN COUNTRIES: GREAT BRITAIN, FRANCE, RUSSIA, UNITED STATES) VS. AXIS POWERS (MAIN COUNTRIES: GERMANY, ITALY, JAPAN)

THE VICTOR: ALLIES

CASUALTIES: ALLIES—14,141,544 DEAD; AXIS—5,634,232 DEAD

An Air Force bomber pilot speaks to his crew during World War II.

SERGEANT JOHN FOLEY

John Foley joined the Army Air Forces in November 1941. Just one month later, the United States entered World War II after Japan attacked Pearl Harbor. Without even going through basic training, Foley shipped out to an airbase in Brisbane, Australia.

Foley's main job at the base was cleaning the bomber guns. One of those bombers was a B-26 flown by Lieutenant Walter Krell. When Krell's turret gunner got injured, he started looking for a replacement. Krell liked Foley's work on the guns so he asked if Foley could take the job.

Foley got a crash course on using the gun turret. With only a day and a half of training, he flew into combat. It turned out he was a natural with the weapon. Foley shot down a Japanese Zero fighter plane on his very first mission. Two weeks later he took down two more Zeros.

Sergeant John Foley (center, kneeling) with the other crew members of his B-26 bomber.

A war reporter heard about Foley and nicknamed him "Johnny Zero." Soon the heroism of "Johnny Zero" caught people's attention back in the United States. A hit song called "Johnny Got a Zero" even made

Foley (right) serving as an instructor at the AAF Gunnery School in Fort Myers, Florida.

it onto the radio. Foley was famous. Meanwhile Foley kept fighting. He shot down at least seven more planes in 32 missions. He also survived three crashes, one of which he was the only survivor.

In 1943 Foley caught malaria and returned to the United States. After a brief time as a gunnery instructor, he shipped out to England to fight as a B-24 gunner. He completed 31 missions in just 60 days. Still eager to fight, Foley volunteered for a third tour. Just as he was preparing to go, the war ended.

TECHNICAL SERGEANT ARIZONA HARRIS

On January 3, 1943, Arizona Harris controlled the top turret of a B-17 named the Sons of Fury. This bomber was among 84 others on a mission to destroy Japanese submarines off the western coast of France. On the way there, antiaircraft fire blasted the Sons of Fury and three other bombers.

Bullets ripped through the Sons of Fury. Two engines shut down and the nose of the aircraft was blown away. Seriously wounded, the pilot and navigator did everything they could to control the bomber. Meanwhile, Harris took aim at six German fighters trying to blow the Sons of Fury out of the sky.

a formation of B-17 bombers during World War II

About 40 miles (64 km) off the French coast, the Sons of Fury belly-landed in the Bay of Biscay. As the bomber sank, Harris continued firing his gun until his turret finally slipped beneath the waves. For his bravery fighting to the very end, Harris was posthumously awarded the Distinguished Service Cross.

A B-17 bomber helps destroy an aircraft factory in northern Poland during World War II.

THE KOREAN WAR

DATES: 1950–1953

THE COMBATANTS: UNITED STATES, SOUTH KOREA, AND UNITED NATIONS (UN) VS. NORTH KOREA AND CHINA

THE VICTOR: NO VICTOR; THE UN AND NORTH KOREA SIGNED A TRUCE, BUT NO PERMANENT PEACE TREATY WAS EVER SIGNED BY NORTH KOREA AND SOUTH KOREA

CASUALTIES: UNITED STATES, UN, AND SOUTH KOREA—256,631 DEAD; CHINA AND NORTH KOREA—ESTIMATED 1,006,000 DEAD

A group of F-86E Sabre fighter jets patrols the skies above Korea in 1953.

CAPTAIN MANUEL FERNANDEZ

Captain Manuel Fernandez never passed up a chance to fly during the Korean War. Between September 1952 and August 1953, he flew 124 combat missions and took out at least 14 enemy fighters. But his actions on March 21, 1953, best display his rank as the third-best flying ace of the war.

While flying over North Korea, Fernandez spotted a formation of 30 enemy fighters. Although heavily outnumbered he went on the attack. During his approach he tried dropping his extra fuel tanks to increase his speed. But only one tank dropped, limiting how well his plane could fly. Rather than give up the chase, he pushed ahead and caught up to the last two enemy fighters.

Fernandez opened fire on the two fighters. He peppered one fighter's wing and body with bullets. As he prepared for another attack, the second fighter attacked him. Fernandez quickly circled around and locked onto his attacker. With several quick bursts of gunfire, he took out the second fighter, causing its pilot to eject.

Fernandez then hunted down the first fighter he had hit. As he closed to within 150 feet (46 meters), his gunfire sent the fighter spiraling to the ground. For his courage in Korea, Fernandez earned the Distinguished Service Cross and the Silver Star.

THE VIETNAM WAR

DATES: 1959–1975

THE COMBATANTS: UNITED STATES, SOUTH VIETNAM, AND THEIR ALLIES VS. NORTH VIETNAM AND ITS ALLIES

THE VICTOR: NORTH VIETNAM

CASUALTIES: UNITED STATES–58,220 DEAD; SOUTH VIETNAM–ESTIMATED 200,000 TO 250,000 DEAD; NORTH VIETNAM–ESTIMATED 1.1 MILLION DEAD

An AC-47 gunship flies over South Vietnam during the Vietnam War.

AIRMAN FIRST CLASS JOHN LEVITOW

On February 24, 1969, John Levitow flew on an AC-47 gunship during a night mission over South Vietnam. He was part of a crew dropping flares into a combat zone. These flares helped ground troops locate enemy positions.

Suddenly an enemy mortar blasted a 2-foot (0.6-m) hole in the wing of the plane. More than 40 pieces of burning shrapnel tore through Levitow's back and legs. Although bleeding and in pain, he helped move another injured man away from the open cargo door. Then he noticed a smoking flare among spilled ammunition on the aircraft floor.

In an instant Levitow realized the live flare was about to ignite. He tried to grasp it with his hands but couldn't get a grip. Finally he threw himself on top of the flare and hugged it to his body. Then he slid to the back of the plane and shoved it out the cargo door. As the flare spun away through the air, it flashed white-hot. Levitow's quick thinking had saved the aircraft and his crew. For his bravery, he received the Medal of Honor.

CAPTAIN LANCE SIJAN

On November 9, 1967, Captain Lance Sijan and Colonel John Armstrong flew a bombing run over Laos. As they released their payload, the bombs exploded early and engulfed their F-4C Phantom fighter-bomber in flames. Armstrong died instantly, but Sijan ejected from the fiery wreck.

Sijan's parachute dropped him in the jungle below. Although he had escaped the crash, Sijan still suffered serious injuries. His right hand and left leg were broken. He had a fractured skull and deep cuts on his body. On top of that, he had no food and very limited survival gear.

The next day a search and rescue team picked up Sijan's distress signal. Although they tried several times, heavy enemy fire made a rescue impossible. The rescue mission was called off. Sijan was considered missing in action (MIA).

F-4C Phantom fighter-bomber

A group of F-4C Phantom fighter-bombers drops bombs over North Vietnam in 1966.

Despite his injuries, Sijan dragged himself 3 miles (4.8 km) through the dense jungle. He survived for 45 days before being captured. In his prison cell, two other American prisoners of war (POWs) tried to mend Sijan's injuries. But his body never had a chance to heal. He was beaten and tortured on a regular basis. Through it all, he never gave up military secrets. Even though he was weak and injured, Sijan's will to survive remained strong. He even talked to fellow prisoners about plans for escape. But he eventually caught pneumonia and died on January 22, 1968.

For his courage and will to survive, Sijan was posthumously awarded the Medal of Honor. The Air Force further honored Sijan by creating the Lance P. Sijan Award. It honors Air Force men and women who show exceptional leadership.

OPERATION ENDURING FREEDOM

DATES: 2001–PRESENT

THE COMBATANTS: AFGHANISTAN GOVERNMENT, THE UNITED STATES AND ITS COALITION FORCES VS. AL-QAIDA TERRORIST ORGANIZATION AND THE TALIBAN, AN ISLAMIC GROUP THAT SUPPORTS AL-QAIDA

THE VICTOR: CONFLICT ONGOING

CASUALTIES: AMERICAN AND COALITION FORCES (THROUGH DECEMBER 6, 2012)–3,215 DEAD; AFGHAN CIVILIANS (REPORTED FROM JANUARY 2007 TO JUNE 2012)–13,009 DEAD; TALIBAN AND AL-QAIDA–NUMBER UNKNOWN

Senior Airman Mark Forester with a group of Afghan children

SENIOR AIRMAN MARK FORESTER

On September 29, 2010, Mark Forester joined a team of Army Special Forces soldiers and Afghan National Army soldiers. Their mission was to attack insurgents in Jangalak Village. As they entered the village, heavy gunfire erupted. In order to call in air support, Forester put himself in the line of fire. But his efforts paid off when two attack helicopters provided cover for the team to reach a safer position.

As the battle raged on, a bullet fatally injured one of the Army soldiers. Forester immediately led a small group into enemy fire to retrieve him. During the rescue a bullet ripped through Forester's chest. Though fatally wounded, he continued to fight until his last breath. In the end Forester's actions helped take out 12 insurgents. The remaining members of the team were able to capture a stockpile of weapons and ammunition. For his bravery and sacrifice, Forester was posthumously awarded the Silver Star.

TECHNICAL SERGEANT ANGELA BLUE

In June 2011 Angela Blue deployed to Forward Operating Base Sweeny in Afghanistan. As an aeromedical technician, her job was to help treat and evacuate soldiers wounded in battle.

Only one month after arriving, Blue's base came under attack. Grenades, mortars, and heavy machine gun fire pounded the compound. Blue received a radio call to help with injuries on the Afghan National Army side of the base. When she got there, she helped wounded soldiers while the base was still under attack. As she worked she noticed one patient bleeding beneath the tourniquet on his leg. She immediately put a second tourniquet on the leg to stop the bleeding. Blue's quick thinking saved his life.

Toward the end of her tour, Blue and her team traveled with Afghan soldiers on a resupply mission. Suddenly one of the Afghan Humvees hit a bomb called an improvised explosive device (IED). Blue raced to the scene to help the injured. While her team treated the soldiers with less serious wounds, she helped the more seriously wounded driver. Because of her team's quick action, everyone in the Humvee survived.

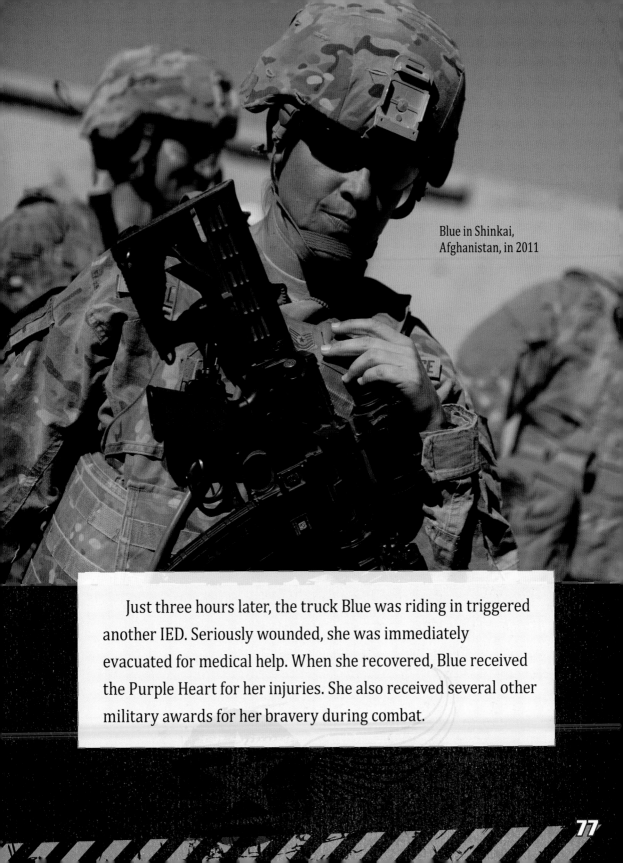

Blue in Shinkai, Afghanistan, in 2011

Just three hours later, the truck Blue was riding in triggered another IED. Seriously wounded, she was immediately evacuated for medical help. When she recovered, Blue received the Purple Heart for her injuries. She also received several other military awards for her bravery during combat.

STAFF SERGEANT BEN SEEKELL

On May 8, 2011, Ben Seekell and his military working dog, Charlie, joined a security mission. As they returned to Bagram Airfield, they stepped on a land mine. The ground exploded, sending Seekell and Charlie sailing through the air. Not aware that his leg was almost completely torn off, Seekell tried calling out to members of his team. He was especially worried about his canine partner. Charlie suffered several shrapnel wounds and cowered in terror from the noise.

Seekell faced a long, painful recovery. He had five surgeries, which included the amputation of his foot. He also struggled through about five hours of intense physical therapy every day. But Seekell was determined to work with Charlie again. Only eight months after losing his foot, he passed the Air Force fitness test. Seekell once again returned to active duty with Charlie at his side.

Seekell receives a visit from his working dog, Charlie, four months after becoming injured in Afghanistan.

STAFF SERGEANT ROBERT GUTIERREZ JR.

On October 5, 2009, Robert Gutierrez Jr. was working with an Army Special Forces unit. Their task was to take out a Taliban target in a small village in Afghanistan's Herat province. As a combat controller, Gutierrez's job was to call in air support during the mission.

As the unit entered the village, they came under heavy fire. When a fellow soldier's rifle jammed, Gutierrez jumped into his place. He took a bullet to the chest that collapsed his lung. The searing pain made it nearly impossible for him to breathe.

The unit's medic plunged a 7-inch (18-centimeter) needle into Gutierrez's chest to blow his lung back up. Then Gutierrez called in an F-16 and a gunship to clear out the enemy fighters firing on them.

Because of Gutierrez's actions, no U.S. soldiers were killed during the battle. For his bravery and heroism, he earned the Air Force Cross.

Gutierrez in
Afghanistan

OPERATION IRAQI FREEDOM

DATES: 2003–2011

THE COMBATANTS: THE UNITED STATES AND COALITION FORCES VS. IRAQ, FIRST THE GOVERNMENT OF SADDAM HUSSEIN AND THEN INSURGENTS

THE VICTOR: THE UNITED STATES DEFEATED SADDAM HUSSEIN IN 2003 BUT THEN FACED STIFF FIGHTING FROM INSURGENTS UNTIL ITS WITHDRAWAL IN 2011

CASUALTIES: AMERICAN AND COALITION FORCES—4,804 DEAD; IRAQI SOLDIERS AND INSURGENTS—ESTIMATED MORE THAN 30,000 DEAD

An A-10 Thunderbolt II aircraft flies over Iraq in 2006.

CAPTAIN KIM CAMPBELL

On April 7, 2003, Captain Kim Campbell flew her A-10 Thunderbolt II over Baghdad, Iraq. She was providing air support to ground troops when a massive jolt rocked her aircraft. An enemy surface-to-air missile had hit the tail of her fighter. Campbell recalled, "There was no question ... I knew I had been hit by enemy fire." The jet rolled left and pointed toward the ground. It didn't respond to any of Campbell's control inputs.

Campbell quickly used the manual override to gain control of the aircraft. The jet leveled off and she managed to fly back to the airbase. But Campbell knew landing would be difficult. Gripping the controls and remembering her flight training, she landed the crippled aircraft perfectly. For her courage that day Campbell received the Distinguished Flying Cross.

Campbell's heavily damaged A-10 Thunderbolt II

U.S. MARINES
TRUE
STORIES

ALWAYS FAITHFUL

The Marine Corps traces its roots back more than 200 years. This branch of the U.S. military got its start on November 10, 1775. At that time it was called the Continental Marines. During the Revolutionary War, the Continental Marines fought on both land and sea. They were often the first soldiers to face the enemy in battle.

When the Revolutionary War ended, the United States no longer needed as much protection. The Continental Marines disbanded. But as the United States quickly grew, so did the threats to the new nation. In 1798 President John Adams brought the Marine Corps back to help the Navy. Ever since, the Marines have fought in every major U.S. war. Though a separate branch, it remains under Navy command to this day.

The Marine Corps' motto, Semper Fidelis, is Latin for "Always Faithful." No matter where duty takes them, Marines hold this motto close to their hearts. They are faithful to their fellow soldiers, their country, and their fight for freedom.

WORLD WAR I

DATES: 1914–1918

THE COMBATANTS: ALLIES (MAIN COUNTRIES: GREAT BRITAIN, FRANCE, ITALY, RUSSIA, UNITED STATES) VS. CENTRAL POWERS (MAIN COUNTRIES: GERMANY, AUSTRIA-HUNGARY, BULGARIA, OTTOMAN EMPIRE)

THE VICTOR: ALLIES

CASUALTIES: ALLIES–5,142,631 DEAD; CENTRAL POWERS–3,386,200 DEAD

Marines clash with the Germans in the Battle of Belleau Wood during World War I.

CAPTAIN GEORGE HAMILTON

On June 6, 1918, Captain George Hamilton led his Marines in the Battle of Belleau Wood. This battle in the wooded hills of France was one of the bloodiest of World War I. Using darkness for cover, Hamilton's mission was to clear the Germans from a hilltop 800 yards (732 m) away.

At 3:45 a.m. Hamilton and his troops advanced on the German line. Almost immediately they faced heavy machine gun fire. "We hadn't moved 50 yards when [the Germans] cut loose at us from the woods ahead," Hamilton later recalled. "[It was] more machine guns then I had ever heard before."

Pinned to the ground, Hamilton crawled on his belly. He encouraged any able Marines to follow him as he weaved in and out of the woods. Then they darted across a field and entered another wooded area. As enemy fire rained down, Hamilton and his men rushed over the hill. He used his bayonet to bring down German soldiers blocking his path. The hole he created in the German line allowed more Marines to rush in. By the end of the day, they had taken control of the hill. For his courage Hamilton earned the Navy Cross and two Distinguished Service Crosses.

WORLD WAR II

DATES: 1939–1945

THE COMBATANTS: ALLIES (MAIN COUNTRIES: GREAT BRITAIN, FRANCE, RUSSIA, UNITED STATES) VS. AXIS POWERS (MAIN COUNTRIES: GERMANY, ITALY, JAPAN)

THE VICTOR: ALLIES

CASUALTIES: ALLIES—14,141,544 DEAD; AXIS—5,634,232 DEAD

Marines battle a fire in an aircraft hangar at Henderson Field on the island of Guadalcanal in November 1942.

GUNNERY SERGEANT JOHN BASILONE

During World War II, the United States battled the Japanese in the Pacific Ocean. By late 1942, U.S. forces had captured Henderson Field on the island of Guadalcanal. Sergeant John Basilone was one of the Marines charged with defending the airbase from the Japanese.

On October 24 about 3,000 Japanese soldiers attacked Basilone's position. Fighting in rain and mud, Basilone and his 15 men defended their position from two machine gun stations.

Heavily outnumbered, the two-day battle didn't go well for Basilone and his men. When the Japanese took out one of the gun stations, only Basilone and two other Marines remained able to fight. But he didn't give up. Basilone lifted his 100-pound (45-kilogram) machine gun and ran to the empty gun station. From there he hammered away at the endless enemy attacks.

When his ammunition ran low, Basilone armed himself with a pistol. He dashed for a supply area now behind enemy lines. He grabbed all the ammo he could carry and raced back to the gun station. After fighting through a second night, the Japanese finally withdrew. Basilone and his men had protected Henderson Field. He earned the Medal of Honor for his actions.

COLONEL PETER ORTIZ

Peter Ortiz was born in the United States and moved to France as a child. In 1939 he joined the French Foreign Legion. This branch of the French army allowed foreigners living in France to fight in World War II. In 1940 Ortiz was shot in the leg and captured by the Germans. During 15 months in prison camps, he attempted several escapes. Finally, in October 1941, he was successful and made his way to the United States. Less than a year later, he enlisted in the Marines and headed back to war.

While stationed in North Africa, Ortiz was assigned to the Office of Strategic Services (OSS). He worked with secret agents from England and France. In January 1944 the group parachuted into France. They met up with French Resistance members fighting against the Nazis controlling the country.

Ortiz and his men moved often, keeping their location secret. One night Ortiz disguised himself and entered a café in a German-occupied town. He overheard a Nazi comment on "the filthy American swine" that were helping the French Resistance. The comment angered Ortiz. He shed his costume and confronted the Nazis with a pistol in each hand. Guns blazing, Ortiz took out the Nazis and fled the scene.

In August 1944 the Germans spotted Ortiz and other Marines in the small town of Centron. Ortiz and the other Marines bolted. They hid in the homes of friendly French townspeople. But Ortiz knew that if they didn't surrender, the Nazis would hurt the residents. After talking to his fellow Marines, they agreed to turn themselves in. They spent the rest of the war in a prison camp, but the townspeople were left unharmed.

Peter Ortiz arrives in New York in 1941 after having escaped from a German prison camp.

After the war Ortiz was released from prison and he returned to the United States. For his bravery during the war he earned two Navy Crosses, the Legion of Merit, and two Purple Hearts.

THE KOREAN WAR

DATES: 1950–1953

THE COMBATANTS: UNITED STATES, SOUTH KOREA, AND UNITED NATIONS (UN) VS. NORTH KOREA AND CHINA

THE VICTOR: NO VICTOR; THE UN AND NORTH KOREA SIGNED A TRUCE, BUT NO PERMANENT PEACE TREATY WAS EVER SIGNED BY NORTH KOREA AND SOUTH KOREA

CASUALTIES: UNITED STATES, UN, AND SOUTH KOREA–256,631 DEAD; CHINA AND NORTH KOREA–ESTIMATED 1,006,000 DEAD

First Lieutenant Baldomero Lopez (top) leads the charge over the seawall in the Battle of Inchon.

FIRST LIEUTENANT BALDOMERO LOPEZ

When the Korean War began, North Korea won some of the early battles. But within a few months, UN forces began pushing back. Win or lose, they knew the Battle of Inchon on September 15, 1950, would be critical. UN forces needed a stronghold near North Korea, and Seoul, the South Korean capital, was close to Inchon. First Lieutenant Baldomero "Punchy" Lopez was part of the risky invasion to eventually retake Seoul.

When Lopez and his platoon landed in Inchon, the beach exploded with enemy fire. The wide-open beach left the men totally exposed. Using ladders, Lopez led his men over a towering seawall. With bullets buzzing by, Lopez topped the wall first. Once over, he spotted an enemy bunker. Lopez grabbed a hand grenade and yanked out the pin. As he wound up to throw, bullets tore into his chest and right shoulder. The live grenade tumbled out of his hand.

Severely injured, Lopez crawled toward the grenade. He tried to grasp it but couldn't. He knew he must get the grenade away from his men. With seconds left, he pulled the grenade under his body. The blast killed Lopez instantly, but his sacrifice saved the other Marines. A war reporter later said, "... [Lopez] died with the courage that makes men great." Lopez posthumously received the Medal of Honor for his sacrifice.

THE VIETNAM WAR

DATES: 1959–1975

THE COMBATANTS: UNITED STATES, SOUTH VIETNAM, AND THEIR ALLIES VS. NORTH VIETNAM AND ITS ALLIES

THE VICTOR: NORTH VIETNAM

CASUALTIES: UNITED STATES–58,220 DEAD; SOUTH VIETNAM–ESTIMATED 200,000 TO 250,000 DEAD; NORTH VIETNAM–ESTIMATED 1.1 MILLION DEAD

Marines fire their weapons during the Vietnam War.

PRIVATE FIRST CLASS ROBERT RIMPSON

On August 18, 1965, Private First Class Robert L. Rimpson took part in Operation Starlite. It was the first major battle the United States fought on the ground in Vietnam. It was also a day that changed 19-year-old Rimpson's life forever.

Rimpson and his fellow soldiers had orders to advance on an enemy trench. Suddenly intense gunfire began cutting them down. Wounded soldiers dropped all around him. But Rimpson pushed forward. He fired his rifle and grenade launcher into the trench as fast as he could.

Robert Rimpson in 2013

After clearing the trench line, Rimpson discovered he was wounded. A shard of shrapnel had struck near his eye. But Rimpson didn't give up. With blurry vision, he helped more seriously wounded soldiers reach a rescue helicopter. At the same time, he fired grenades at the enemy. His actions allowed more rescue helicopters to land and take off safely.

After the war Rimpson received a Purple Heart for his injuries. In May 2013 he was also awarded the Bronze Star. After the ceremony Rimpson said, "I've never been more proud to be a Marine."

Rimpson holds up his citation for the Bronze Star during the award ceremony in May 2013.

LANCE CORPORAL NED SEATH

In 1966 Lance Corporal Ned Seath led a machine gun team in Vietnam. Deep in enemy territory, their mission was to block enemy trails running through the jungle.

On July 16 Seath and his men were attacked at night. His key gunner was wounded and a bullet had damaged the soldier's weapon. In total darkness Seath crawled to the injured Marine. He grabbed the broken machine gun and quickly took the weapon apart. Then he did the same with another broken weapon. Suddenly a mortar shell exploded nearby. It wounded his hand and leg. But Seath continued putting the pieces of the two weapons together to build one working firearm. Then he stood up, returned fire, and slowed down the attack.

Ned Seath (right) receives the Navy Cross in 2011.

In 2011 Seath received the Navy Cross for his actions that day in Vietnam. At the ceremony Bill Hutton, who fought with Seath, recalled, "If it weren't for Ned Seath, I'd be buried right now ... in Arlington [National Cemetery]. He went above and beyond the call of duty. He saved a company of Marines."

OPERATION DESERT STORM

DATES: 1991

THE COMBATANTS: UNITED STATES AND COALITION FORCES VS. IRAQ

THE VICTOR: UNITED STATES AND COALITION FORCES

CASUALTIES: AMERICAN AND COALITION FORCES—1,065 DEAD; IRAQ—20,000–35,000 DEAD

An Iraqi tank burns after an attack during Operation Desert Storm.

CORPORAL MICHAEL KILPATRICK

In early 1991, 22-year-old Corporal Michael Kilpatrick experienced two action-packed days while serving during Operation Desert Storm. On February 14 he was driving a support vehicle near Kuwait when it came under heavy mortar fire. Thinking quickly he managed to speed out of harm's way. Then he called in air strikes to take out the attackers.

The very next day, Kilpatrick spotted two Iraqi tanks and about 40 soldiers in the distance. They were heading toward him and fellow Marine Bryan Zickefoose. Rather than retreat, the two men decided to head off the attack on their battalion. Armed with rocket launchers, they charged toward the tanks. As they closed in, each fired a rocket, and they took out both tanks. Then their battalion regrouped and surrounded the Iraqis.

Both Kilpatrick and Zickefoose received Silver Stars for their bravery. Kilpatrick shrugged off his actions. He said, "Somebody saw me doing my job and thought it was special for some reason." Kilpatrick dedicated his award to his father, who died in the Vietnam War in 1969.

OPERATION ENDURING FREEDOM

DATES: 2001–PRESENT

THE COMBATANTS: AFGHANISTAN GOVERNMENT, THE UNITED STATES AND ITS COALITION FORCES VS. AL-QAIDA TERRORIST ORGANIZATION AND THE TALIBAN, AN ISLAMIC GROUP THAT SUPPORTS AL-QAIDA

THE VICTOR: CONFLICT ONGOING

CASUALTIES: AMERICAN AND COALITION FORCES (THROUGH DECEMBER 6, 2012)–3,215 DEAD; AFGHAN CIVILIANS (REPORTED FROM JANUARY 2007 TO JUNE 2012)–13,009 DEAD; TALIBAN AND AL-QAIDA–NUMBER UNKNOWN

U.S. Marines on patrol as they battle Taliban forces in Afghanistan in 2008.

FIRST LIEUTENANT REBECCA TURPIN

On December 13, 2008, First Lieutenant Rebecca Turpin led her platoon on a supply mission to Musa Qala, Afghanistan. About seven hours into the mission, an improvised explosive device (IED) hit one of the vehicles in her convoy. Turpin ordered a quick search for more IEDs in the area. Two were found and disarmed before the convoy moved on.

Eight hours later Turpin's convoy hit another IED in total darkness. But the group pressed forward until they came to a small village. Suddenly Turpin heard one of her gunners yell, "RPG!" Seconds later a rocket-propelled grenade (RPG) hit their refueling truck's engine. Gunfire and grenades hit and disabled another vehicle. Turpin ordered the convoy to surround the disabled vehicles. Her actions shielded her team as they prepared to tow one vehicle and repair the other. Turpin then called for air support to protect the convoy.

After two and a half days, Turpin's convoy reached Musa Qala with zero casualties. Turpin was awarded the Navy and Marine Corps Commendation Medal for her leadership under enemy fire.

CORPORAL DAKOTA MEYER

At a ceremony in 2011, President Barack Obama said, "Dakota [Meyer] is the kind of guy who gets the job done." These words reflect the bravery, determination, and quick thinking of Corporal Dakota Meyer during Operation Enduring Freedom.

On September 8, 2009, a morning patrol of American soldiers and Afghan forces walked into the village of Ganjgal, Afghanistan. Before they could meet with people from the village, Taliban fighters ambushed them.

Dakota Meyer and Sergeant Juan Rodriguez-Chavez were stationed about 1 mile (1.6 km) outside of the village. Over the radio they listened to the commands of their fellow soldiers under attack. They knew the patrol was outnumbered and needed help. They radioed a commanding officer for permission to go in. They were told the situation was too dangerous. They asked three more times and were still denied.

Corporal Dakota Meyer stands near the village of Ganjgal in Afghanistan.

Meyer and Rodriguez-Chavez decided they had to act. Meyer said, "Those were my brothers, and I couldn't just sit back and watch." They hopped in a military vehicle and charged into the battle zone. Meyer fired the gun on top of the vehicle and picked up wounded soldiers along the way. When the vehicle was full, they drove to safety and unloaded the wounded. Then they went back in for another load. On the fourth trip, hot shrapnel tore into Meyer's arm. On the fifth, they found a group of four fallen Marines. Through heavy fire, they carried each soldier's body to their vehicle.

Because of their bravery, 23 Afghan allies and 13 Americans survived the attack. Meyer received the Medal of Honor and Rodriguez-Chavez received the Navy Cross for their courage.

Meyer enjoys a quiet moment in the village of Ganjgal, Afghanistan.

SERGEANT RYAN SOTELO

Sergeant Ryan Sotelo served in the 3rd Battalion, 5th Marine Regiment during Operation Enduring Freedom. His unit had more casualties than any other during the conflict. More than 160 of its members had been wounded and 25 were killed in combat.

On November 25, 2010, insurgents battered the unit with heavy gunfire. A bullet struck and killed platoon commander First Lieutenant William Donnelly almost immediately. Without hesitation, Sotelo took control of the unit. He led troops to a nearby canal for better cover. The unit was safer, but Sotelo didn't stay put for long. He raced back into the gunfire to retrieve his fallen officer.

As he ran Sotelo saw an insurgent firing at his men. He darted toward him while activating a grenade. As he closed in, he tossed the weapon and killed the insurgent. Then he grabbed Donnelly's body and returned to the canal.

As the fighting continued, Sotelo knew they could not win. He slowly withdrew the troops, fighting until they were all safely behind the American line. Sotelo received the Silver Star for his leadership and quick judgment while under fire.

OPERATION IRAQI FREEDOM

DATES: 2003–2011

THE COMBATANTS: THE UNITED STATES AND COALITION FORCES VS. IRAQ, FIRST THE GOVERNMENT OF SADDAM HUSSEIN AND THEN INSURGENTS

THE VICTOR: THE UNITED STATES DEFEATED SADDAM HUSSEIN IN 2003 BUT THEN FACED STIFF FIGHTING FROM INSURGENTS UNTIL ITS WITHDRAWAL IN 2011

CASUALTIES: AMERICAN AND COALITION FORCES—4,804 DEAD; IRAQI SOLDIERS AND INSURGENTS—ESTIMATED MORE THAN 30,000 DEAD

U.S. Marines clear out houses held by insurgents in Fallujah, Iraq, in 2004.

FIRST SERGEANT BRADLEY KASAL

All Marines believe in the Semper Fi motto. But for some, the promise to be "Always Faithful" shows most in the heat of battle. Such was the case for First Sergeant Bradley Kasal during Operation Iraqi Freedom.

In 2004 Kasal was stationed in Fallujah, Iraq. While helping his platoon, an explosion of gunfire rang from an Iraqi home. Kasal knew that several troops were inside. As soldiers ran from the house, Kasal charged in. While helping a wounded Marine to safety, bullets tore through both of his legs.

Medical supplies ran low quickly. With only enough to bandage one of the wounded Marines, Kasal refused medical treatment.

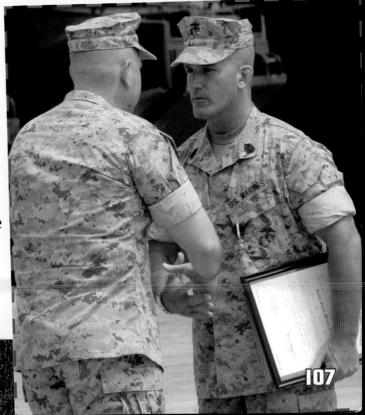

Kasal receives the Navy Cross for his actions in Iraq.

Meanwhile, the insurgents hadn't quit. One tossed a grenade, hoping it would force the Marines to come out of hiding. It rolled within a few feet of the men. Sacrificing his safety, Kasal threw himself between the grenade and the other Marines. His courageous actions saved several of his fellow Marines. When the battle ended, Kasal had been hit by seven rounds of ammo and more than 40 pieces of shrapnel.

Kasal survived his wounds—but just barely. By the time he arrived at a hospital, he had lost 60 percent of his blood. He needed 20 surgeries to save his legs. After recovering, Kasal walked with a limp. But he returned to work as Sergeant Major of the School of Infantry (West) at Camp Pendleton in Southern California. He earned a Navy Cross and a Purple Heart for his actions in Iraq.

Kasal (right) talks with fellow Marines about leadership after a presentation at Camp Pendleton.

Marines patrol the streets of Haqlaniyah, Iraq, in a LAV-25 armored personnel carrier.

DIRECT QUOTES

Page 10 from "Sergeant William H. Carney" by Jane Waters, New Bedford Historical Society (www.nbhistoricalsociety.org/sgtcarney.html).

Page 11 from "Richard Kirkland, 'The Humane Hero of Fredericksburg'" by General J. B. Kershaw (www.civilwar.org/education/history/primarysources/richard-kirkland.html).

Page 13 from The Diary of Alvin York by Alvin C. York (http://acacia.pair.com/Acacia.Vignettes/The.Diary.of.Alvin.York.html).

Page 19 from The Permanent Book of The 20th Century: Eye-Witness Accounts of the Moments that Shaped Our Century edited by Jon E. Lewis (New York: Carroll & Graf, 1994).

Page 23 from the Congressional Medal of Honor Society (www.cmohs.org/recipient-detail/3173/pililaau-herbert-k.php).

Page 27 from "Face of Defense: Woman Soldier Receives Silver Star" by Micah E. Clare, U.S. Department of Defense (www.defense.gov/news/newsarticle.aspx?id=49348).

Page 31 from "Capt. Carter's War: Test of Courage, Decency" by Chris Tomlinson, Los Angeles Times (http://articles.latimes.com/2003/apr/27/news/adfg-captcarter27).

Page 35 from The Monitor Boys: The Crew of the Union's First Ironclad by John V. Quarstein (Charleston, S.C.: The History Press, 2011).

Page 36 from Reign of Iron: The Story of the First Battling Ironclads, the Monitor and the Merrimack by James L. Nelson (New York: HarperCollins, 2004).

Page 42 from "Cook Third Class Doris Miller, USN" Naval History & Heritage Command (www.history.navy.mil/faqs/faq57-4.htm).

Page 75 from "Operation Iraqi Freedom Hero Shares Her Story" by Stacie N. Shafran, U.S. Air Force (www.af.mil/News/ArticleDisplay/tabid/223/Article/117270/operation-iraqi-freedom-hero-shares-her-story.aspx).

Page 87 from George W. Hamilton, USMC: America's Greatest World War I Hero by Mark Mortensen (Jefferson, N.C.: McFarland & Company, 2011).

Page 90 from "Colonel Peter Julien Ortiz: OSS Marine, Actor, Californian" by Benis Frank (California State Military Museum, www.militarymuseum.org/Ortiz.html).

Page 93 from Marine Corps Decade Timeline (www.marines.com/history-heritage/timeline).

Page 96 from "Decades Later, Marine Awarded for Heroism in Vietnam" by Jeffery Cordero (9th Marine Corps District, www.9thmcd.marines.mil/News/NewsArticleDisplay/tabid/4722/Article/142522/decades-later-marine-awarded-for-heroism-in-vietnam.aspx).

Page 97 from "Marine Receives Navy Cross for Actions in Vietnam War" by Christofer P. Baines (U.S. Department of Defense, www.defense.gov/News/NewsArticle.aspx?ID=62788).

Page 99 from "Persian Gulf War Hero Shares Silver Star with Pilot Killed in Vietnam—His Dad Ceremony: Pennsylvanian was 2 Months Old When Father Went Off to War" Deseret News, July 3, 1991 (www.deseretnews.com/article/170774/PERSIAN-GULF-WAR-HERO-SHARES-SILVER-STAR-WITH-PILOT-KILLED-IN--VIETNAM---HIS-DAD-CEREMONY.html?pg=all).

Pages 102 and 104 from "Remarks by the President Awarding the Medal of Honor to Sergeant Dakota Meyer" by President Barack Obama (www.whitehouse.gov/the-press-office/2011/09/15/remarks-president-awarding-medal-honor-sergeant-dakota-meyer).

SELECT BIBLIOGRAPHY

Arroyo, Rachel. "Combat Controller Posthumously Awarded Silver Star." Air Force Special Operations Command, June 15, 2012, www.afsoc.af.mil/news/story.asp?id=123306176.

Baines, Christofer P. "Marine Receives Navy Cross for Actions in Vietnam War." U.S. Department of Defense, www.defense.gov/News/NewsArticle.aspx?ID=62788.

Birdwell. Michael. "Sgt. Alvin York," WorldWar1.com, www.worldwar1.com/heritage/sgtayork.htm.

Clare, Micah E. "Face of Defense: Woman Soldier Receives Silver Star." U.S. Department of Defense, March 24, 2008, www.defense.gov/news/newsarticle.aspx?id=49348.

Cordero, Jeffrey. "Decades Later, Marine Awarded for Heroism in Vietnam." 9th Marine Corps District, www.9thmcd.marines.mil/News/NewsArticleDisplay/tabid/4722/Article/142522/decades-later-marine-awarded-for-heroism-in-vietnam.aspx.

Correll, John T. "The Legend of Frank Luke," Air Force Magazine, Vol. 92, No.8, August 2009, www.airforcemag.com/MagazineArchive/Pages/2009/August%202009/0809luke.aspx.

Dockery, Kevin. *Navy Seals: A History Part II—The Vietnam Years.* New York: Berkley Books, 2002.

Frank, Benis. "Colonel Peter Julien Ortiz: OSS Marine, Actor, Californian." California State Military Museum, www.militarymuseum.org/Ortiz.html.

Frisbee, John L. "Valor: Unsung Heroes of World War II," Vol. 76, No. 7, July 1993, www.airforcemag.com/MagazineArchive/Pages/1993/July%201993/0793valor.aspx.

Fuentes, Gidget. "3/5 Sergeant to be Awarded Silver Star." Marine Corps Times, March 23, 2012, www.marinecorpstimes.com/article/20120323/NEWS/203230318/3-5-sergeant-awarded-Silver-Star.

Holmstedt, Kirsten. *The Girls Come Marching Home: Stories of Women Warriors Returning from the War in Iraq.* Mechanicsburg, Pa.: Stackpole Books, 2009.

King, Gilbert. "Remembering Henry Johnson, the Soldier Called 'Black Death,'" Smithsonianmag.com, October 25, 2011, www.smithsonianmag.com/history/remembering-henry-johnson-the-soldier-called-black-death-117386701.

Kyle, Chris. *American Sniper: The Autobiography of the Most Lethal Sniper in U.S. Military History.* New York: William Morrow, 2012.

Laster, Jill. "Air Force Senior Airman Mark A. Forester." Military Times, http://projects.militarytimes.com/valor/air-force-senior-airman-mark-a-forester/4819219.

Martin, Iain C. The Greatest U.S. Navy Stories Ever Told. Guilford, Conn.: The Lyons Press, 2006.

Mortensen, Mark. *George W. Hamilton, USMC: America's Greatest World War I Hero.* Jefferson, N.C.: McFarland & Company, 2011.

Nelson, James L. *Reign of Iron: The Story of the First Battling Ironclads, the Monitor and the Merrimack.* New York: William Morrow, 2004.

Patrick, Bethanne Kelly. "Capt. Lance Peter Sijan." Military.com, www.military.com/Content/MoreContent?file=ML_sijan_bkp.

Proser, Jim, and Jerry Cutter. *I'm Staying with My Boys: The Heroic Life of Sgt. John Basilone, USMC.* New York: St. Martin's Griffin, 2010.

Quarstein, John V. *The Monitor Boys: The Crew of the Union's First Ironclad.* Charleston, S.C.: The History Press, 2011.

Shafran, Stacie N. "Operation Iraqi Freedom Hero Shares Her Story," U.S. Air Force, March 18, 2010, www.af.mil/News/ArticleDisplay/tabid/223/Article/117270/operation-iraqi-freedom-hero-shares-her-story.aspx.

Williams, Gary. *Seal of Honor: Operation Red Wings and the Life of Lt. Michael P. Murphy, USN.* Annapolis, Md.: Naval Institute Press, 2010.

Wyckoff, Mac. "Richard Kirland, the Angel of Marye's Heights," Fredericksburg.com, http://fredericksburg.com/CivilWar/Battle/kirkland.htm.